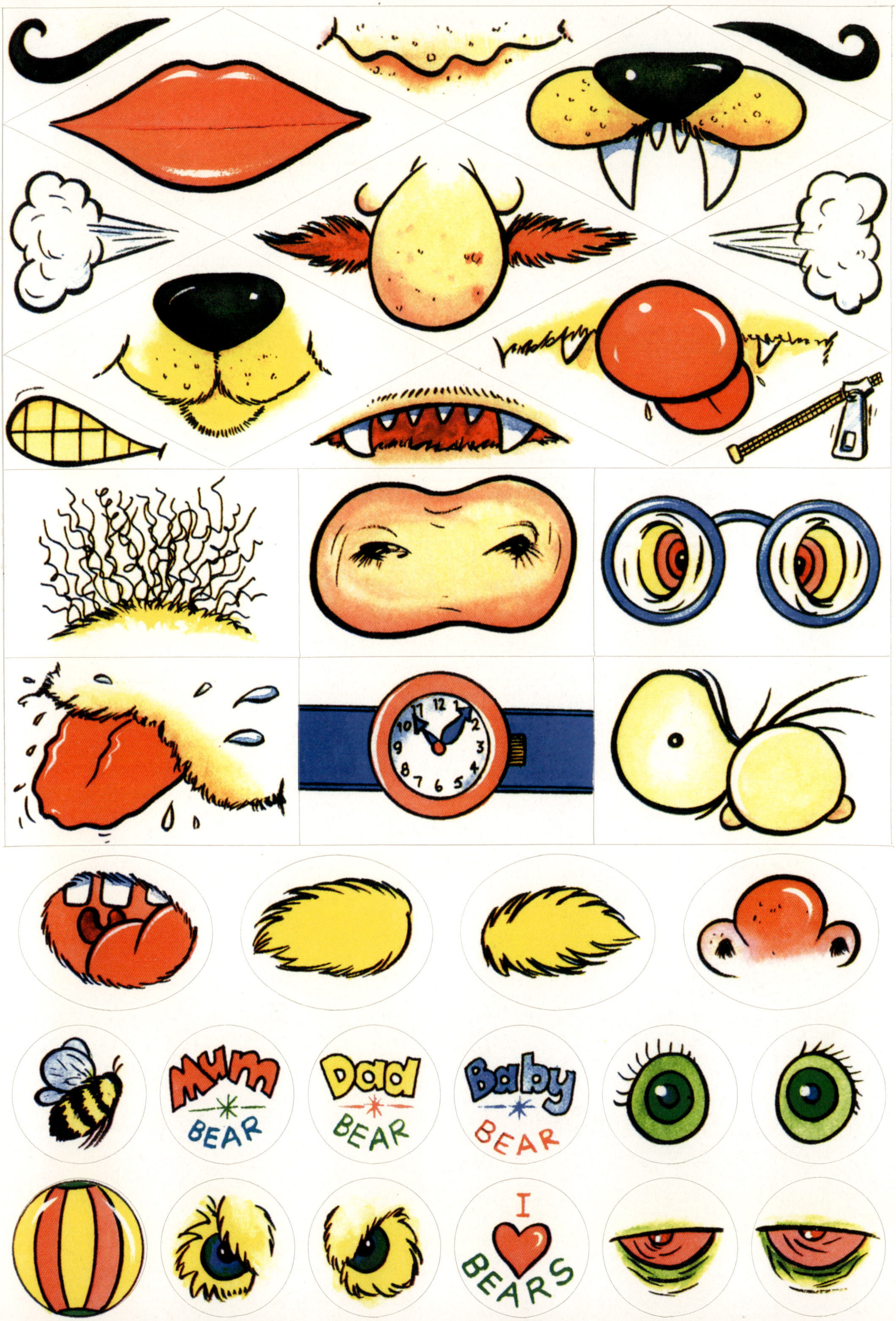
Mum
BEAR
Dad
BEAR
Baby
BEAR
I
BEARS

POLAR BEAR

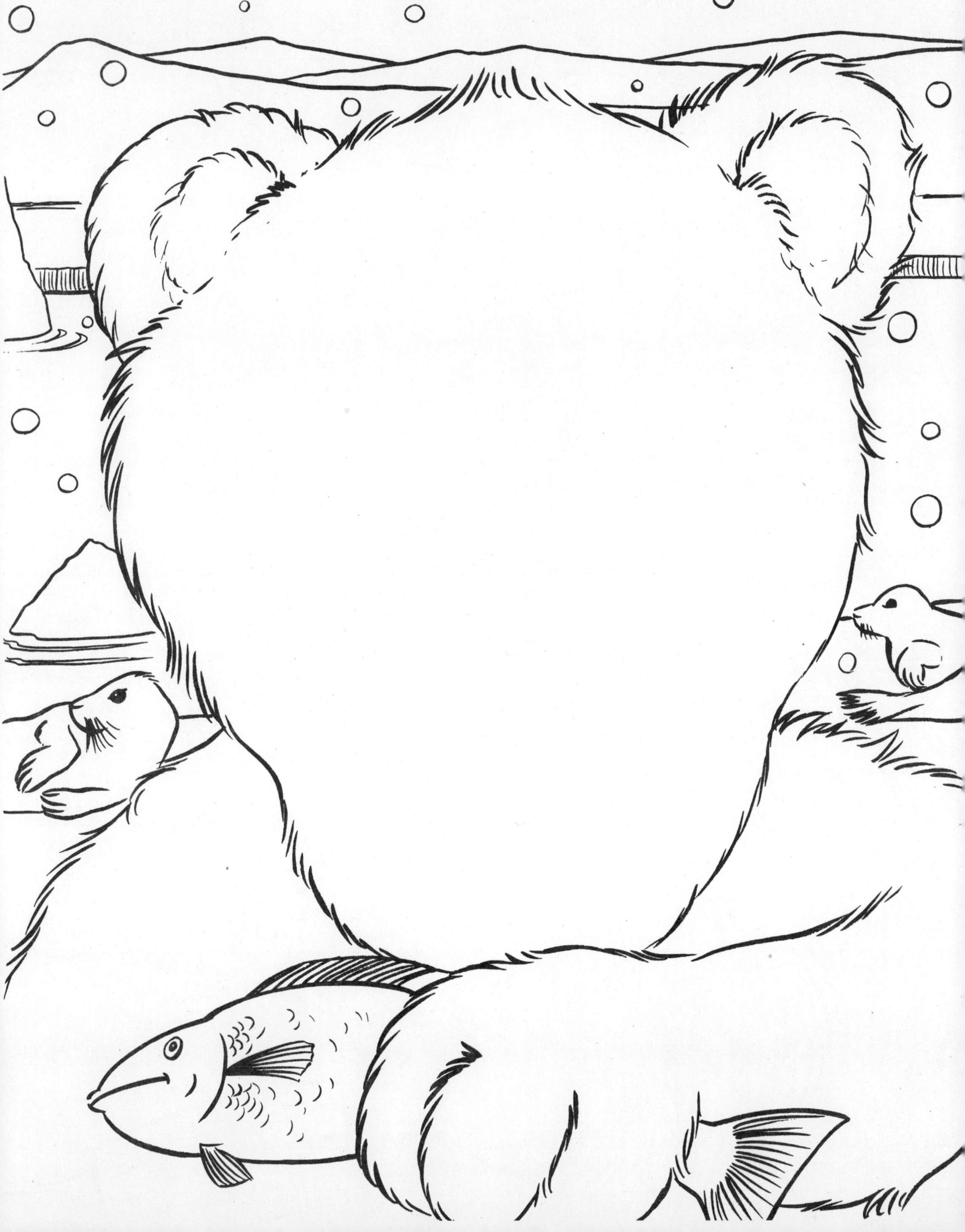

THE THREE BEARS

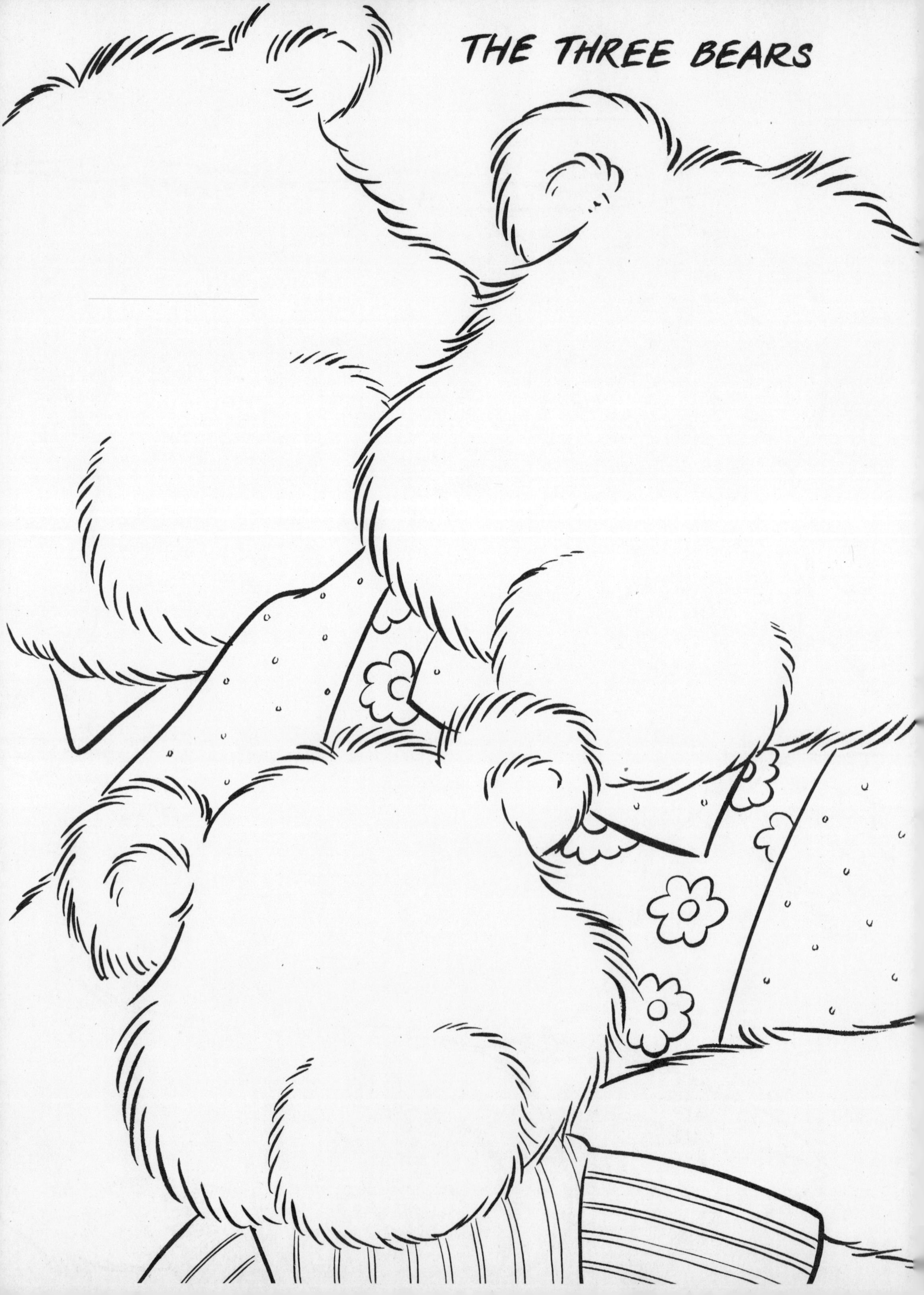

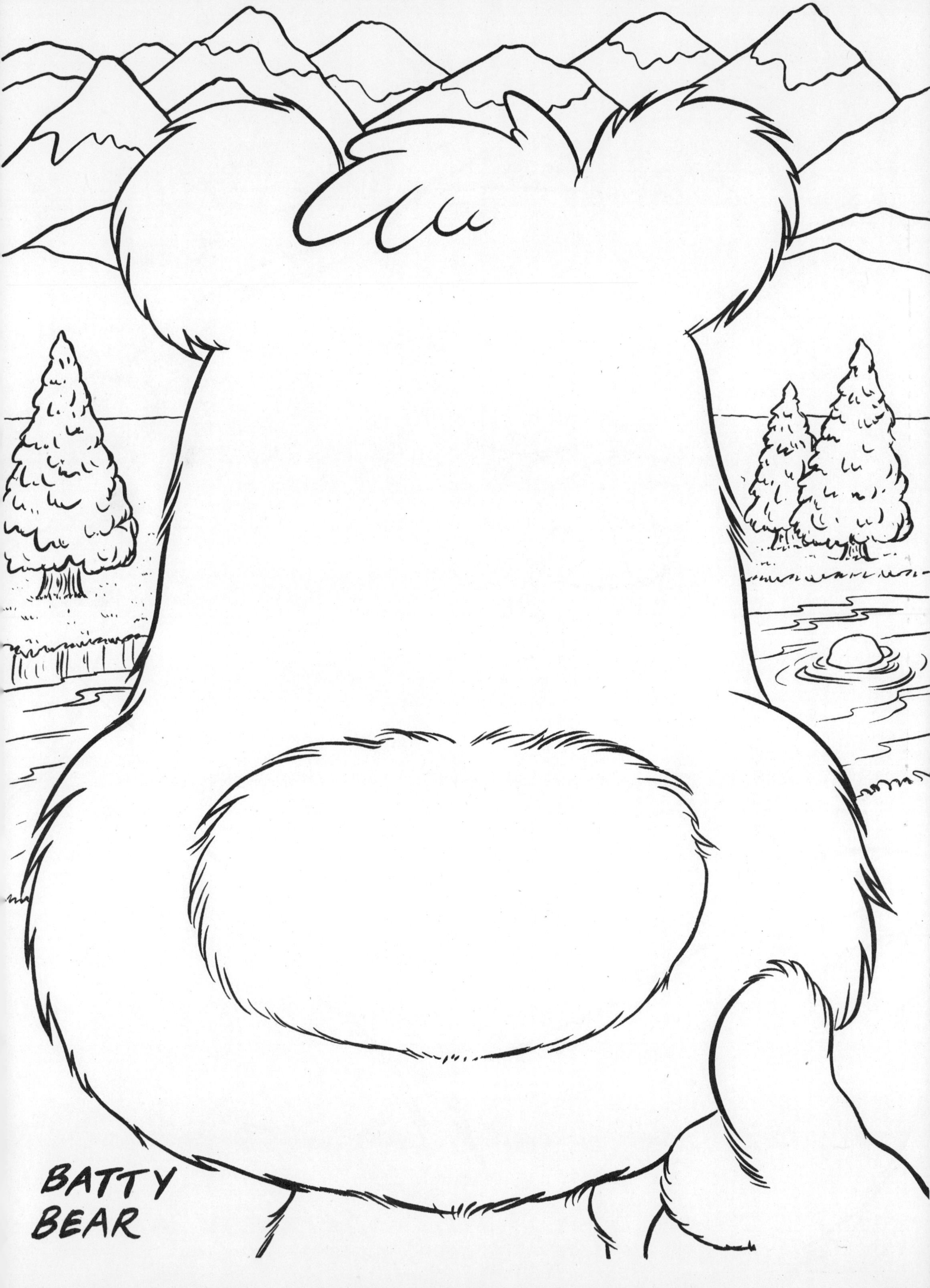
BATTY BEAR

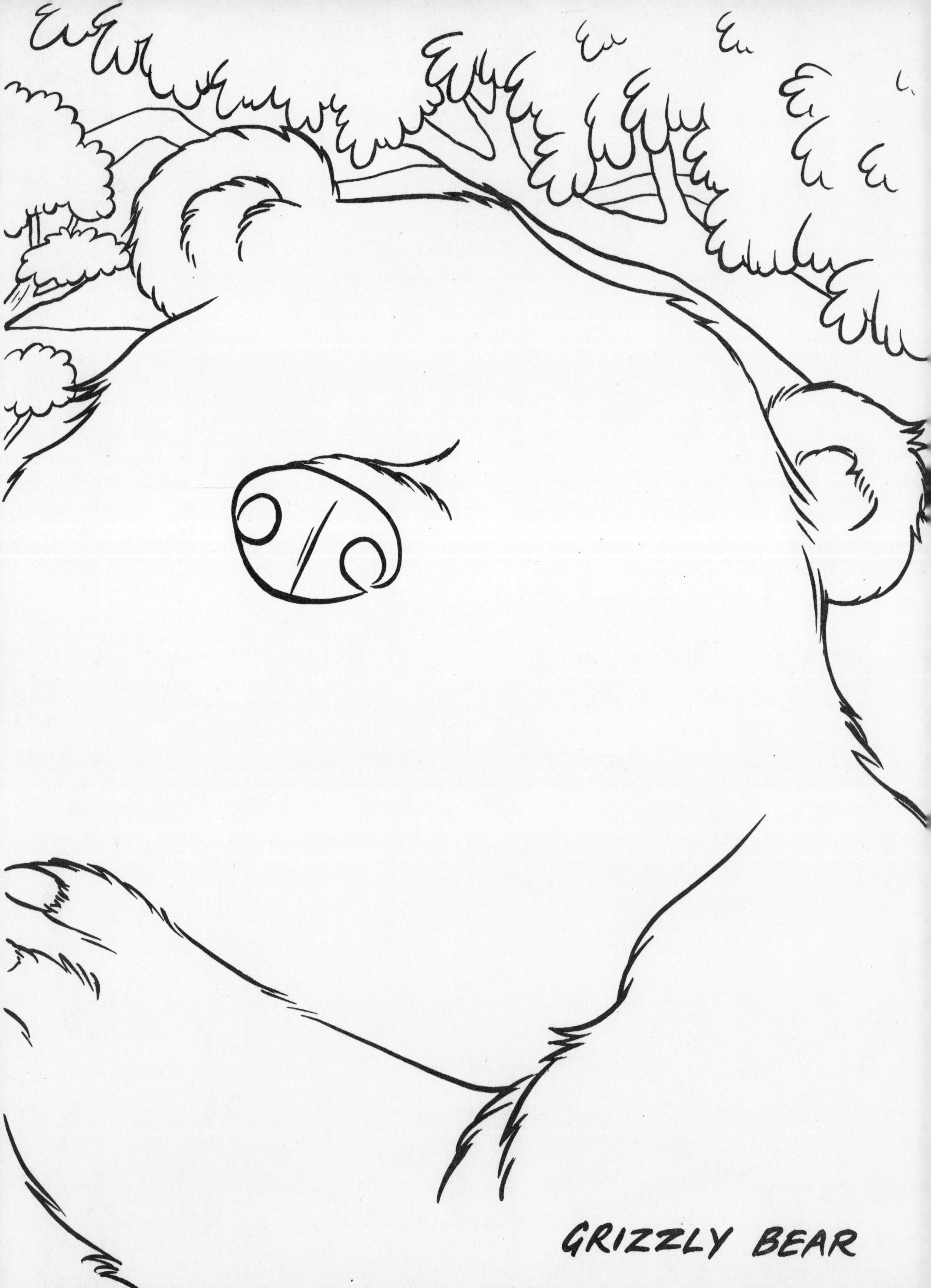

GRIZZLY BEAR

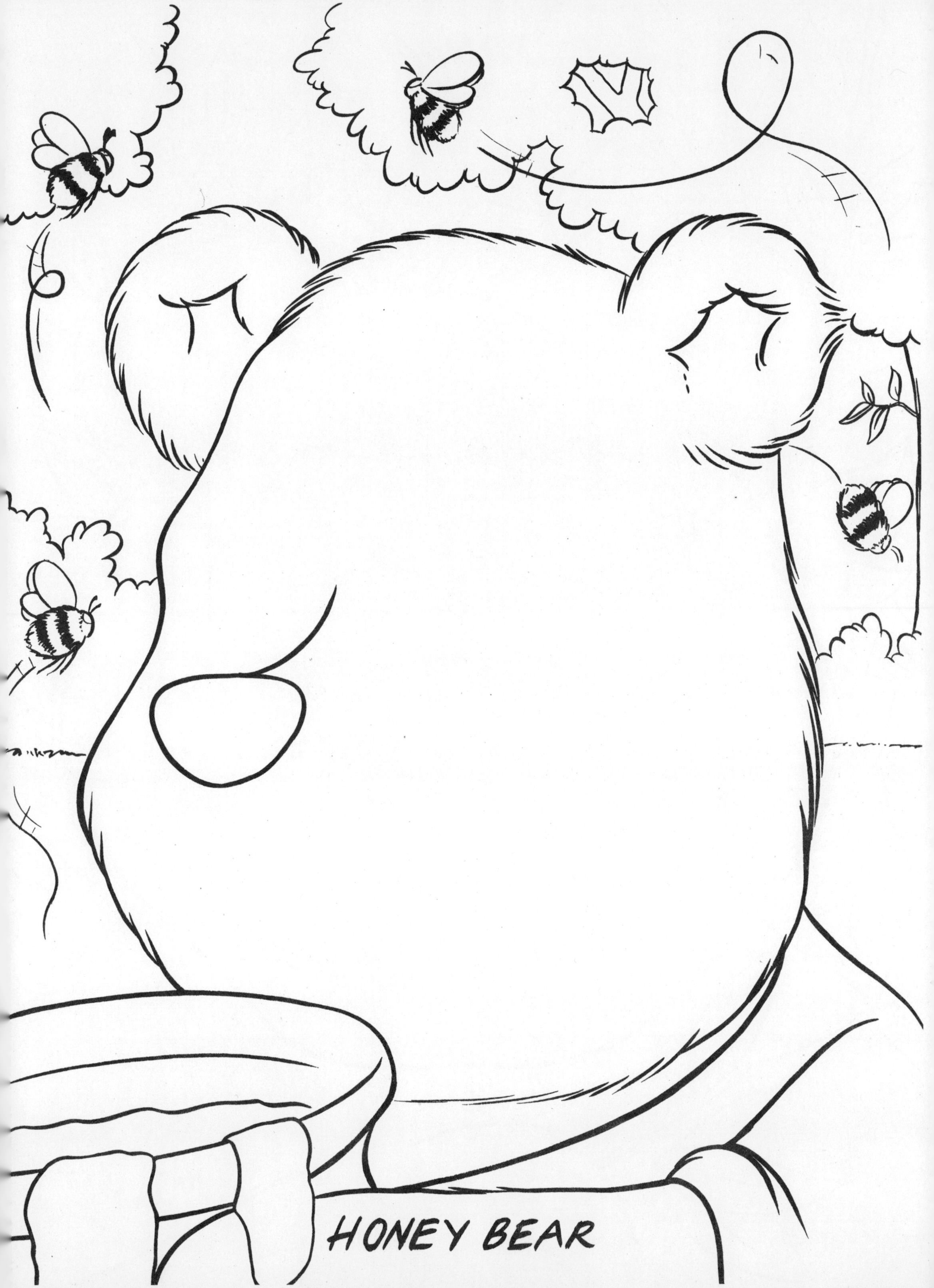

HONEY BEAR

PANDA

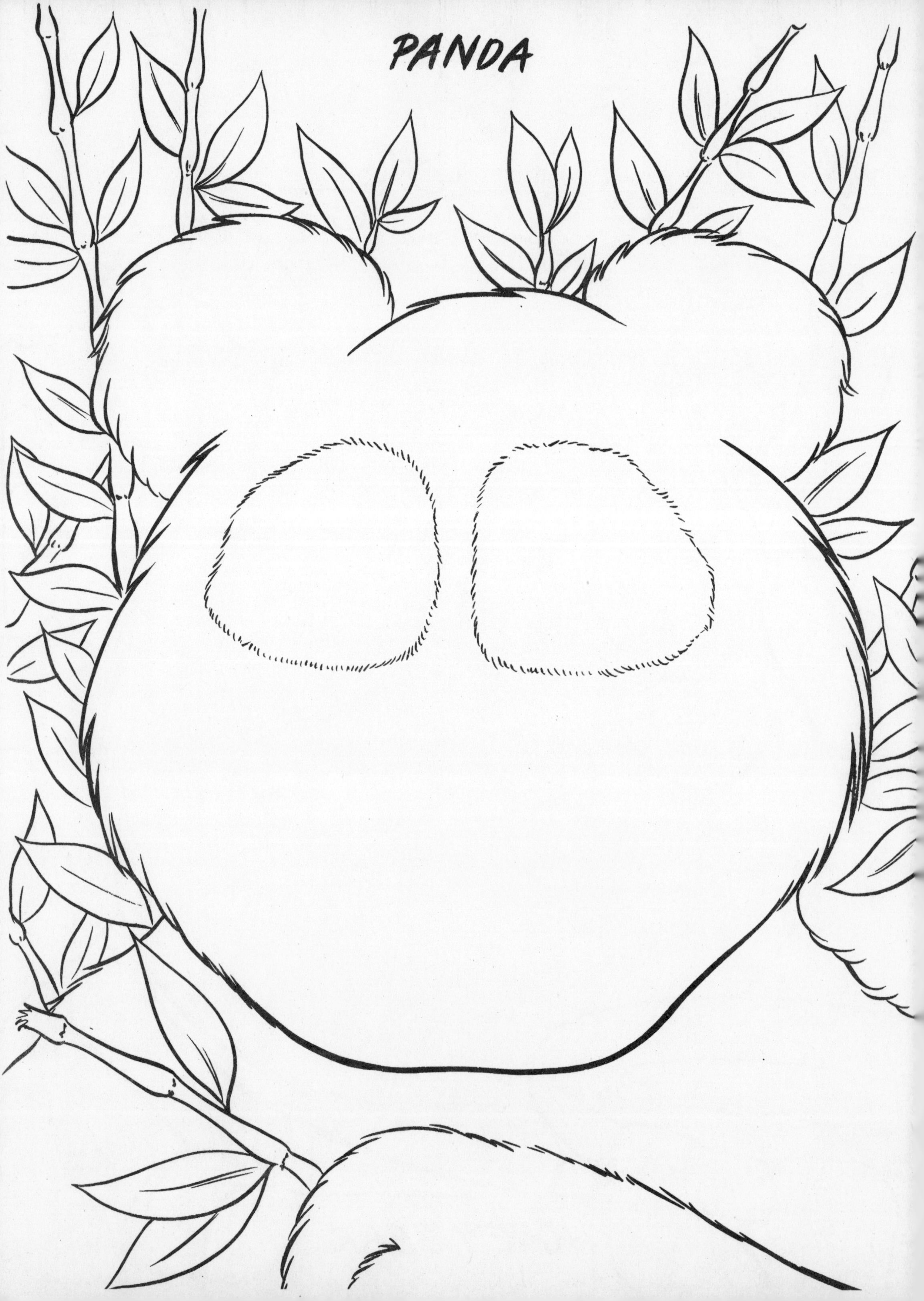

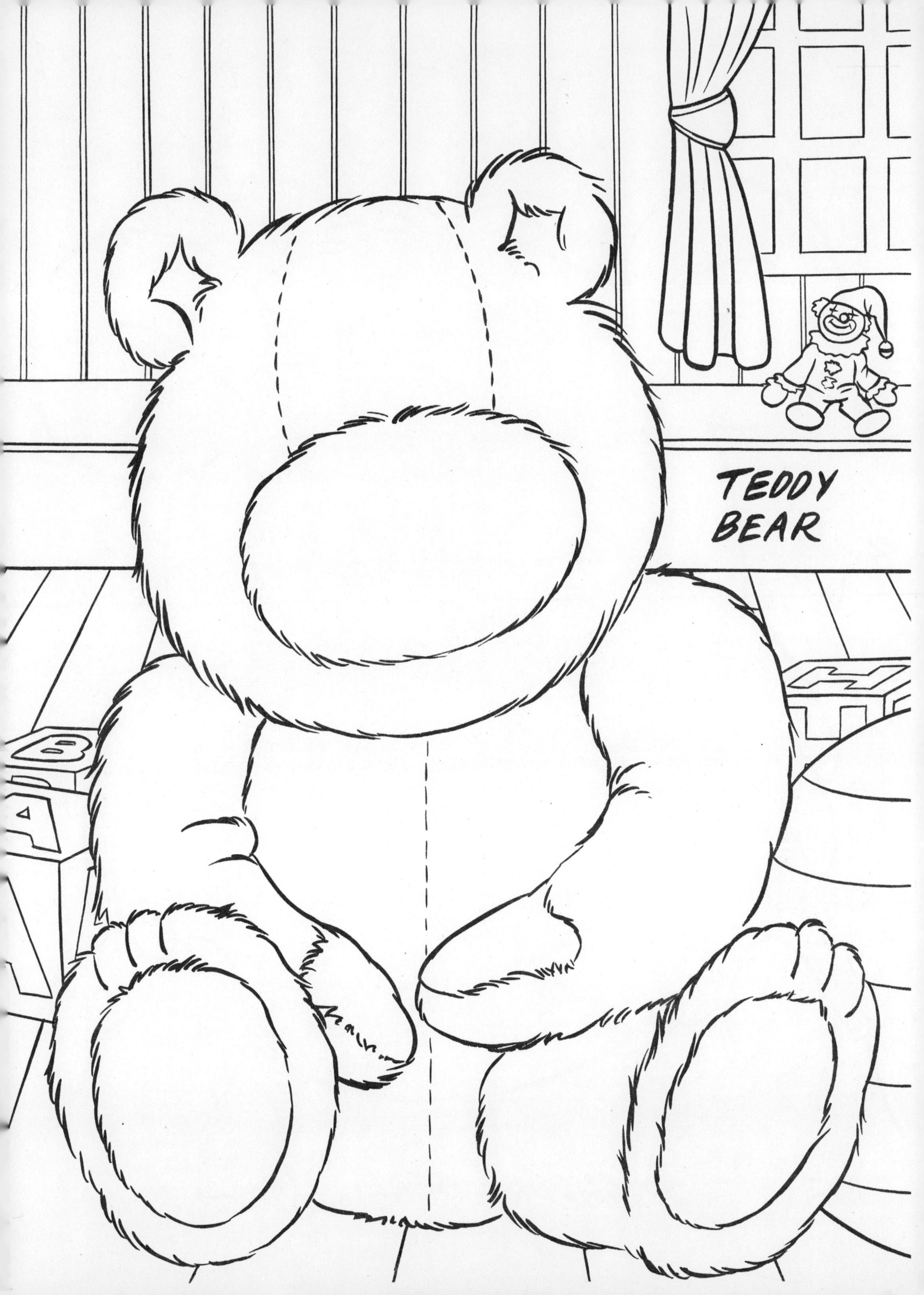
TEDDY
BEAR

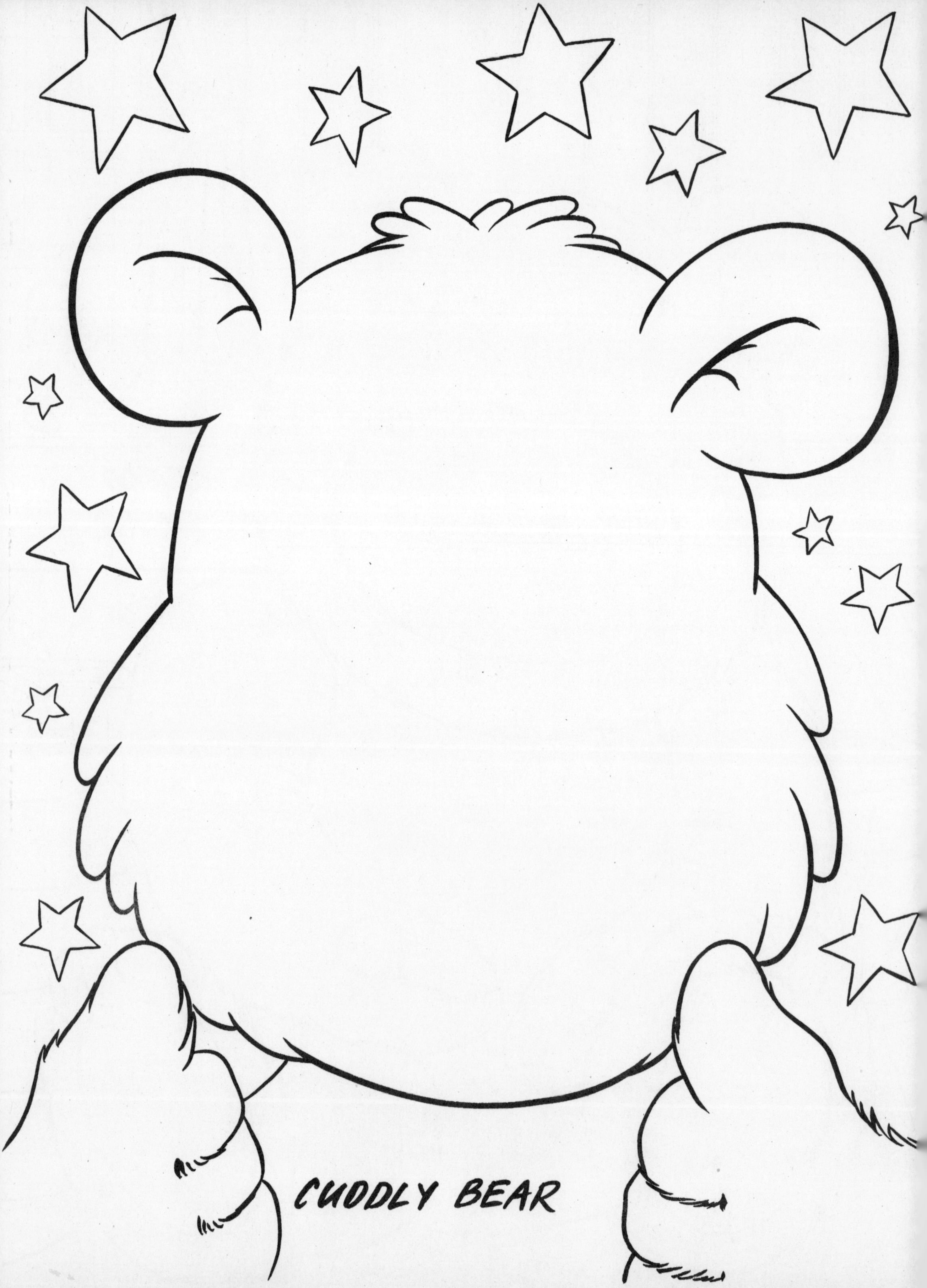
CUDDLY BEAR

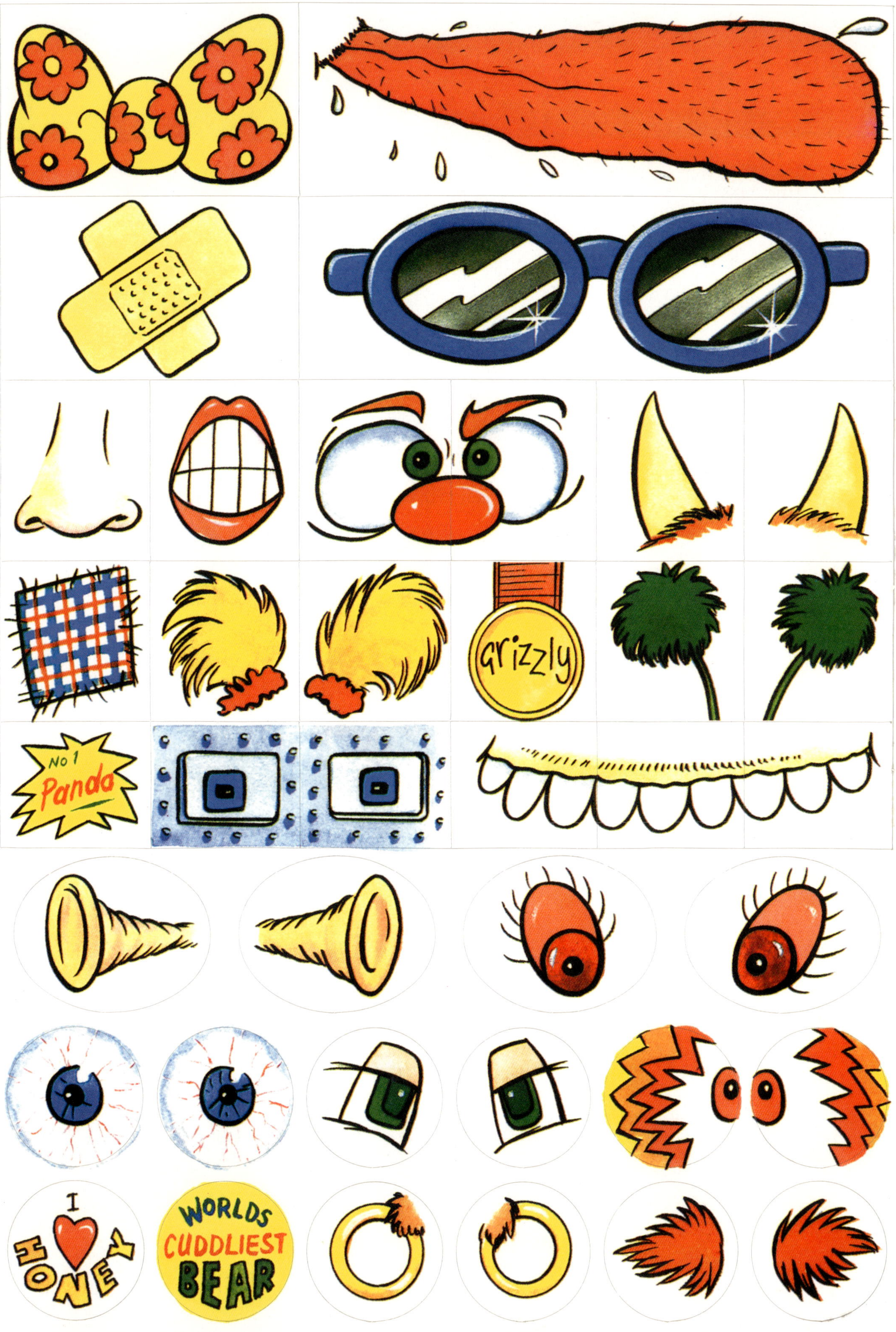
grizzly
No 1
Panda
I
HONEY
WORLDS
CUDDLIEST
BEAR